Easy-to-Make SPACESHIPS That Really Fly

Easy-to-Make
SPACESHIPS
That Really Fly

Mary Blocksma
&
Dewey Blocksma

illustrated by Marisabina Russo

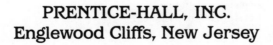

PRENTICE-HALL, INC.
Englewood Cliffs, New Jersey

Text copyright © 1983 by Mary Blocksma and Dewey Blocksma
Illustrations copyright © 1983 by Marisabina Russo

Printed in the United States of America   •J

Prentice-Hall International, Inc., London
Prentice-Hall of Australia, Pty. Ltd., Sydney
Prentice-Hall Canada, Inc., Toronto
Prentice-Hall of India Private Ltd., New Delhi
Prentice-Hall of Japan, Inc., Tokyo
Prentice-Hall of Southeast Asia Pte. Ltd., Singapore
Whitehall Books Limited, Wellington, New Zealand
Editora Prentice-Hall Do Brasil LTDA., Rio de Janeiro

10 9 8 7 6

Book design by Constance Ftera

Library of Congress Cataloging in Publication Data

Blocksma, Mary.
   Easy-to-make spaceships that really fly.

   Summary: Provides directions for spaceships that
can be made without adult supervision from paper
plates, straws, styrofoam cups, and other materials
available in supermarkets. Includes suggestions for
designing one's own spaceships.
   1. Spaceships—Models—Juvenile literature.
1. Space ships—Models.   2. Handicraft   I. Blocksma,
Dewey.   II. Russo, Marisabina, ill.   III. Title.
TL793.B55   1983   629.47'0228   83-10986
ISBN 0-13-223180-8

To our test pilots,
Bruce Schadel
and
Dylan Kuhn

CONTENTS

COUNTDOWN!

Things that fly have a special magic. The earth's air is, after all, the beginning of space. Even your backyard is part of the universe! From there, you can fly into your own science fiction with models you make yourself.

So get ready for blast-off! It won't take long to make some of the spaceships in this book. If you like, you can add on to them. Before long, you will be inventing your own spaceships.

To begin your adventure, find a good place to work. A table or hard floor (not a rug) is best. Cover your work place with newspapers.

WHAT YOU NEED

Tools

You can find the tools you need for your spaceship factory right at home.

A strong pair of *scissors*
A sharp *pencil*
A *stapler (Note:* You don't have to have a stapler, but it will speed up your work.)

Materials

Your supermarket has everything you need. One package of each of these materials will make every model in this book—and more!

Thin, flimsy, white *paper plates*—the kind that curl at the edge
Cold-drink *paper cups*
Regular-size *styrofoam cups*
Cellophane or *masking tape*
Plastic straws that bend
Paste or *glue*

Decorations for the Deep Space Look

No spaceship is complete without some far-out decorations. Here are a few tricks you can use to make your model look as if it just came in from the stars.

1. Collect some space-age materials to use on your model. Metal, styrofoam, and plastic are some good ones that you can probably find right at home.

METAL AND THINGS THAT LOOK LIKE METAL

aluminum foil
bottle caps
gum wrappers

soft drink can pull-tabs
nuts and washers
paper clips

STYROFOAM

fast-food cartons
supermarket meat trays
packing chips

PLASTIC

plastic wrap
picnic knives, spoons, forks
plastic lids
clear "bubble" packaging

2. Cut numbers and letters from printed material to paste on your spaceship. Find them in some of these places.

labels
cereal boxes

old magazines
newspapers

3. Draw, find, or cut out geometric shapes for your spaceship.

4. Use bright colors. Find a big splash of color in a magazine ad or on gift wrap. Cut it into strips, numbers, or interesting shapes to stick on your model. If you have colored tape, use that. (Some tape, called duct tape, is silver.) Paints, markers, or crayons work well, too.

HOW TO FLY YOUR SPACESHIPS

The spaceships in this book fly in two ways—some spin and some fly like jets.

Fling a Spinner!

Spinning spaceships are round, or have been cut from a circle. To fly a spinner, hold it by the edge, like a Frisbee. (The outside edges should curve down.) Bend your elbow and wrist, holding the spinner close to your body. With a snap, straighten your arm and *fling* it!

Pitch a Jet!

Jet spaceships shoot through the air nose-first. To fly one, hold its body between your thumb and second finger, under the wings. Bring the jet behind your shoulder. Then *pitch* it gently, as you might throw a ball.

FLING A SPINNER!   PITCH A JET!

13

STARSHIP

For starters, try making this easy flying star.

What You Need

4 paper plates   scissors
1 plastic straw   pencil
                              tape or stapler

What You Do

1. Draw a star on a paper plate. The star can have 5 or 6 points, but each point must touch the edge of the plate. The star does not have to be perfect.

Step 1

2. Cut out the star. Then trace the star onto 3 more plates. Cut out all the stars.

Step 2

3. Tape or staple all 4 stars into one fat star. Then poke a hole in the middle with the point of your scissors.

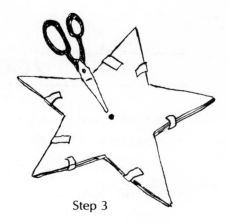

Step 3

4. Poke the plastic straw through the hole.

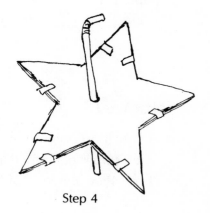

Step 4

Decorate it! To fly it, *fling* it!

ZOOM-A-RANG

The Zoom-a-rang is a basic flying shape. You can fly it by itself, or you can build on it.

What You Need

5 paper plates

scissors
pencil
tape or stapler

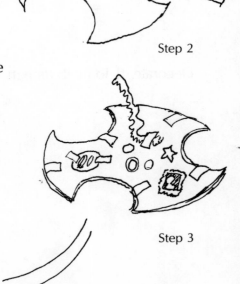

Step 1

What You Do

1. Draw the Zoom-a-rang shape on a paper plate by making 3 horseshoe shapes that touch the edge.

2. Cut out your Zoom-a-rang shape. Then trace it on the other 4 plates. Cut out all the Zoom-a-rang shapes.

3. Match up the pieces. Tape or staple them into one thick Zoom-a-rang.

Decorate it! To fly it, *fling* it!

Step 2

Step 3

SUPER ZOOM-A-RANGS

Your Zoom-a-rang flies just fine. But why stop now? You can add on to your Zoom-a-rang and make it even better!

SUPER ZOOM-A-RANG NUMBER 1 (SZR-1)

What You Need

1 Zoom-a-rang (page 16)   tape
1 paper cup   scissors

Step 1

What You Do

1. Make the cup into a cockpit. Cut some windows in it.

2. Tape the top of the cup to either the top or the bottom of your Zoom-a-rang.

SUPER ZOOM-A-RANG NUMBER 2 (SZR-2)

Step 2

What You Need

1 Zoom-a-rang (page 16)   tape
2 paper cups

What You Do

Tape one cup top to the middle of the Zoom-a-rang. Then tape the second cup to the first, matching the bottoms of the cups.

LANDING GEAR for your ZOOM-A-RANG

Your model does not have to land on its belly. It can land on three legs instead!

What You Need

1 Zoom-a-rang (page 16) scissors
1 styrofoam cup tape
3 bending straws

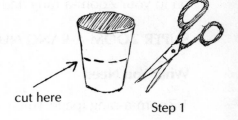

cut here

Step 1

What You Do

1. Cut the styrofoam cup in half around the middle.

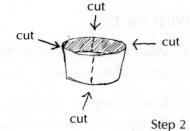

cut

cut

cut

cut

Step 2

2. Cut the ring into four equal pieces.

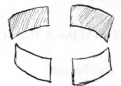

3. Tape one piece to each bending end of the 3 straws. Cut each straw in half. Discard the straight pieces.

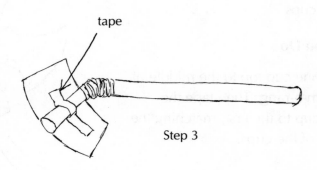

tape

Step 3

4. Tape the straws to the underside of the Zoom-a-rang wings. Use lots of tape.

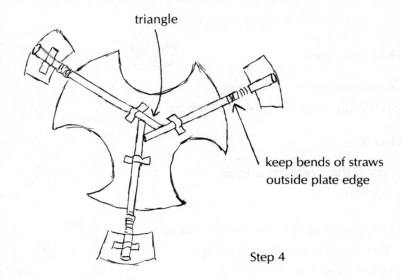

triangle

keep bends of straws outside plate edge

Step 4

5. Now bend the landing gear down, so that the Zoom-a-rang stands on its 3 "feet."

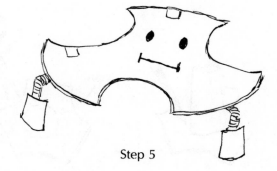

Fly it to a perfect landing!

Step 5

CROWN SPINNER

Believe it or not, there is even *more* you can do with a Zoom-a-rang. You just cut it down to size.

What You Need

1 Zoom-a-rang   scissors
1 styrofoam cup   tape or stapler

What You Do

1. Make the Zoom-a-rang on page 16.

2. Cut the wings off the Zoom-a-rang. You should now have 3 wing pieces and 1 middle piece.

3. Put the big end of the cup down on the middle piece. Trace around the cup. Then cut the circle out. It will fall apart into 5 circles.

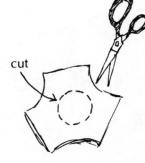

Step 2

Step 3

cut

4. Tape or staple the wings between two of the circles.

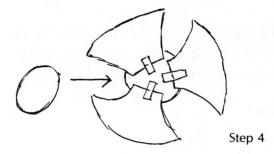

Step 4

5. Draw a crown around the bottom of the cup. Cut out the crown.

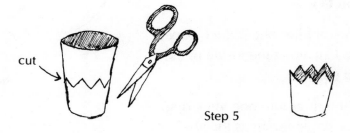

cut

Step 5

6. Tape the crown to the top of the spinner.

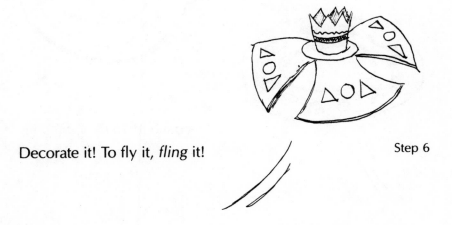

Decorate it! To fly it, *fling* it!

Step 6

ZING RING

The Zing Ring is another basic flying shape. If you're in a hurry, you can make this model in minutes. Or you can go on and make a fancier spaceship from it.

What You Need

6 paper plates

scissors
tape or stapler

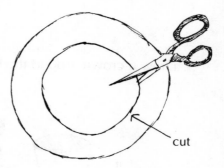

What You Do

1. Cut the middles out of the 6 paper plates. Cut along the inside of the curled edge.

cut

Step 1

2. Stack the rings into one thick ring. Tape or staple the rings together.

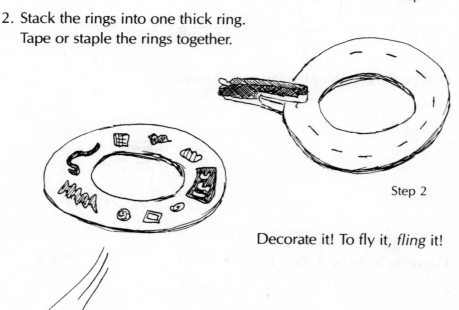

Step 2

Decorate it! To fly it, *fling* it!

FLOATING SAUCER

You can add a whole lot of fancy things to a Zing Ring, and it will still fly! Try a few of these. Then think up some new ones of your own.

What You Need

1 Zing Ring   tape or stapler
1 paper plate

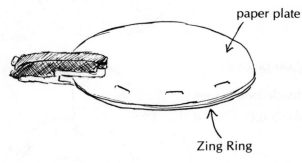

paper plate

Zing Ring

What You Do

1. Make the Zing Ring on page 22.

2. Tape or staple the paper plate on top of the Zing Ring.

Decorate it! To fly it, *fling it!*

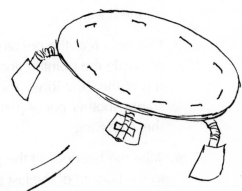

Landing Gear: You might want to add landing gear to your Floating Saucer. To do this, turn to page 18. Follow the directions for making Zoom-a-rang landing gear.

DOUBLE DECKER

This strange spaceship looks a little like
a flying space-age hamburger!

What You Need

1 Zing Ring   scissors
3 paper plates   tape or stapler
                     pencil

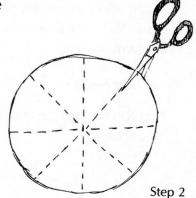

Step 2

What You Do

1. Make the Zing Ring on page 22.

2. With your pencil, divide one paper
   plate into 8 parts, like a pie. Cut on
   all the lines.

3. Use only 6 of the pie pieces. Tape
   or staple the pointed ends to the
   top of the Zing Ring. Then tape or
   staple another paper plate on top of
   the Zing Ring.

4. Tape the big ends of the pie pieces
   to the bottom of the last paper
   plate. Use plenty of tape.

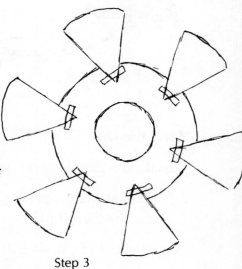

Step 3

Decorate it! To fly it, *fling* it!

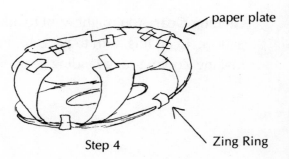

paper plate

Step 4   Zing Ring

WINDOW ZINGER

This spaceship looks harder to make than it is!

What You Need

1 Zing Ring   scissors
2 paper cups   pencil
                   tape or stapler

What You Do

1. Make the Zing Ring on page 22.

2. With your pencil, make five marks on the lip of one of the cups. Space the marks evenly. Now cut from each mark straight down to the bottom of the cup.

3. Bend all the flaps back. Tuck each flap between the layers of the Zing Ring. Tape or staple in place.

4. Tape the second paper cup to the bottom of the first cup.

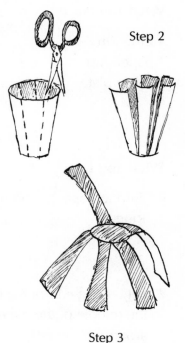

Step 2

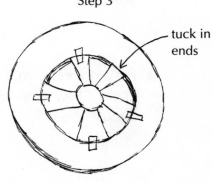

Step 3

tuck in
ends

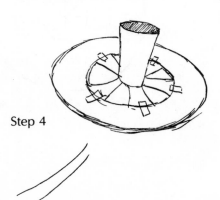

Step 4

Decorate it! To fly it, *fling* it!

COCKPIT FLOATER

This model takes the Zing Ring yet another step!

What You Need

1 Zing Ring   scissors
1 paper cup   pencil
1 paper plate   tape

What You Do

1. Turn to page 22 and make a Zing Ring.

Step 2

2. Set the big end of the cup on the middle of the plate. Draw around it.

3. Put a dot in the middle of the circle. Draw 4 straight lines through the dot.

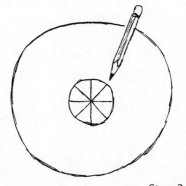

Step 3

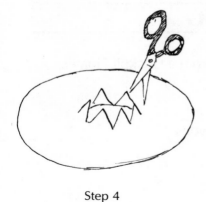

4. Cut on the straight lines. Do not cut past the edge of the circle.

5. Push the bottom of the cup through the hole. Tape the pointed tabs to the cup.

Step 4

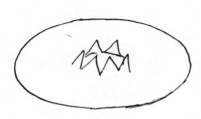

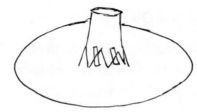

Step 5

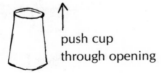

↑ push cup through opening

6. Tape or staple the plate to the Zing Ring.

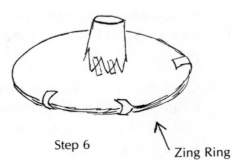

Step 6

↑ Zing Ring

Decorate it! To fly it, *fling* it!

Idea: For an extra-fancy Cockpit Floater, tape a second paper cup to the bottom of the first one.

ZING THING

Scare your friends with this model made from a Cockpit Floater.

What You Need

1 Cockpit Floater   pencil or crayons
3 plastic straws   tape
paper plate scraps

What You Do

1. First make the Zing Ring on page 22. Then make it into a Cockpit Floater (page 26).

2. Turn the Cockpit Floater upside down. Poke the three straws between the cup and the plate of your Cockpit Floater. Tape them in place.

Step 2

3. Cut 3 eyes from the paper plate scraps. Color in some horrible eyeballs. Tape one eye to the end of each straw.

Decorate it! To fly it, *fling* it!

Step 3

ZIP SHIP

The Zip Ship is folded almost the same way as a paper airplane! Instead of spinning, it glides.

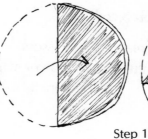
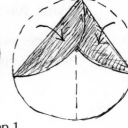

What You Need

1 paper plate   tape
4 regular paper clips or 1 big one

What You Do

1. Fold the plate in half. Open it. Then fold the edges so that they overlap a little at the point.

2. Fold the plate again on the middle fold line, making sure the flaps are on the inside.

Step 1

Step 2

3. Fold one wing back to the middle fold. Do the same with the second wing.

4. Tape the top together. Put 4 small paper clips or 1 big one under the nose.

Step 3

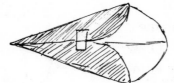

Decorate it! To fly it, *pitch* it!

Step 4

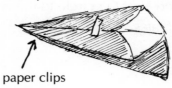

paper clips

29

FLYING FLAPPER

Here is a noisy Zing Ring spaceship!

What You Need

6 paper plates   scissors
1 paper cup   tape or stapler
                  pencil

cut

Step 1

Step 1

Step 2

What You Do

1. Cut the middles out of 3 paper plates. Tape or staple the rings together.

2. Tape or staple the other 3 plates together.

Step 3

3. Set the big end of the cup on the middle of the stapled plates. Draw around it. Now draw 8 lines from the edge of the circle to the edge of the plates.

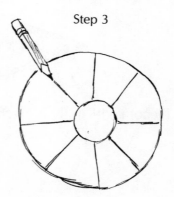

4. Put an X on every other section. Cut the sections *without* any X's into a fringe. Cut only to the edge of the middle circle.

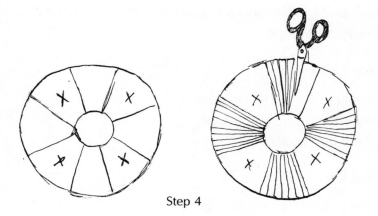

Step 4

5. Tape or staple the fringed plates to the ring. Be sure to fasten them at the X sections only.

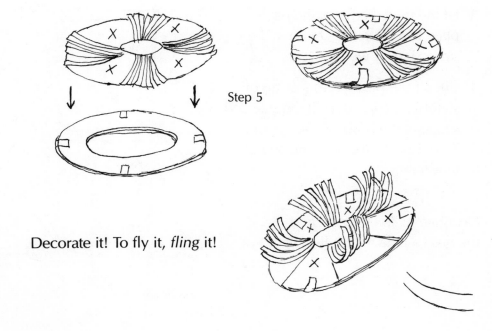

Step 5

Decorate it! To fly it, *fling* it!

MARS-ABOUT

Like the Zip Ship, this model is a jet flyer. It's easy to make and it flies in turns and loops!

What You Need

1 paper plate   scissors
1 bending straw   tape
1 styrofoam cup scrap

What You Do

1. Cut the paper plate in half. Fold one of the half-pieces in half again.

2. Flatten the straight end of the straw. Fold the flat part in half and crease it.

3. Fit the folded edge of the paper plate wing into the crease in the straw. Tape it well.

4. Cut a nose piece from a scrap of styrofoam cup. Make it the size and shape of the bowl of a teaspoon. Tape it *under* the bending end of the straw.

Decorate it! To fly it, *pitch* it! (Bend the nose a little until it flies right.)

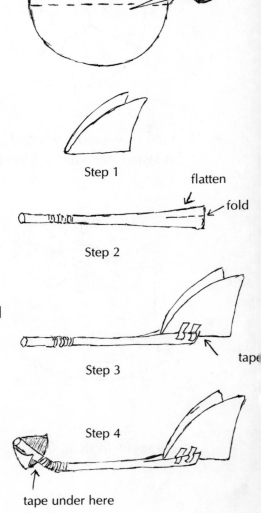

Step 1

flatten

fold

Step 2

Step 3

tape

Step 4

tape under here

GALACTIC GLIDER

This is a most excellent spaceship. It not only looks beautiful—it flies with galactic grace.

What You Need

3 styrofoam cups   scissors
2 bending straws   tape

Step 1

What You Do

1. Cut the bottoms out of the 3 cups.

Step 2

2. Cut two of the cups into 4 pieces.

3. Cut the last cup in half.

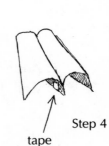

Step 3

4. Tape the cup halves together along one edge to make wings.

tape

Step 4

5. Cut a slit along the straight end of a straw.

Step 5

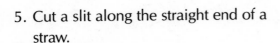

6. Slide the taped bottom edge of the wings into the slit. The straw should reach halfway back along the edge. Tape it in place.

Step 6

Slit the other straw the same way as the first one (see Step 5). Tape it to the wing so that the ends of the straws meet in the middle.

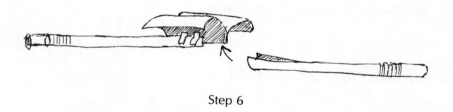

Step 6

7. Add four cup pieces to the wings, two on each side. Tape them well, top and bottom.

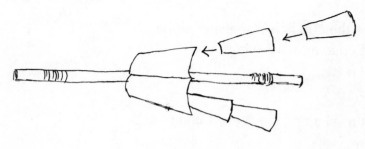

Step 7

8. Tape two more cup pieces together to make the tail. Cut a slit in the top of the tail straw just up to the bend. Slide in the tail and tape well.

   Cut a triangle from a cup scrap for the nose. Tape it in place.

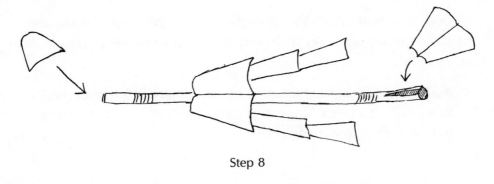

Step 8

9. Round off the wings and tail with scissors. Follow the lines in the drawing.

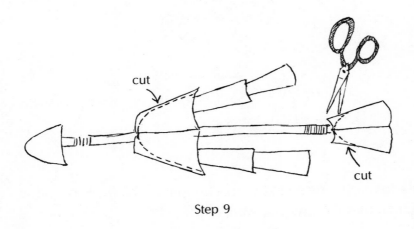

Step 9

Decorate it! To fly it, *pitch* it! (Bend the nose or tail to make it fly right.)

ON YOUR OWN

Once you have made the spaceships in this book, you are ready to make up new ones on your own. Here are some ideas to get you started.

1. Add a square fast-food carton—try one that held a hamburger—to a Floating Saucer. You can put small gifts or secret messages in it, and fly it to a friend.

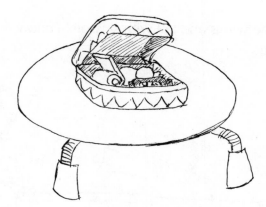

2. Try to make a new kind of spaceship that can fly. Fool with it until it flies the way you want it to.

3. Not all models have to fly. Try making a rocket from cups and straws.

4. Make a really big model to hang from the ceiling of your room. Try stapling a lot of cups together for a moon-base.

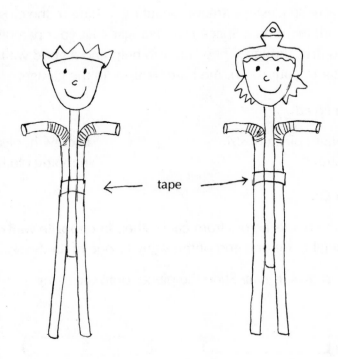

tape

5. Make an astronaut to pilot your Cockpit Floater. Cut two straws in half. Use three of the half-pieces to make a person. Cut out a head, hands, and spacesuit and tape them in place.

SPACE FLEET HANGAR

Surely your spaceships are too beautiful to hide in the closet. Instead, park them on a Space Fleet Hangar. Get your parents' permission first, though. They can also help find a good wall for your hangar in your room, the basement, or in the garage.

What You Need

1 room-length piece of string
8 plastic straws

2 screw hooks
snapping clothespins

What You Do

1. Screw the hooks across from each other, in opposite walls at the same height. Tie one end of the string to one of the hooks.

2. Cut the straws in half. Slide the pieces onto the string.

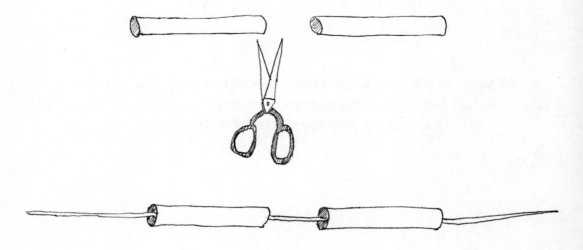

3. Tie the loose end of the string to the second hook. Be sure the string is tight.

4. Clip your spaceships to the straws with clothespins.

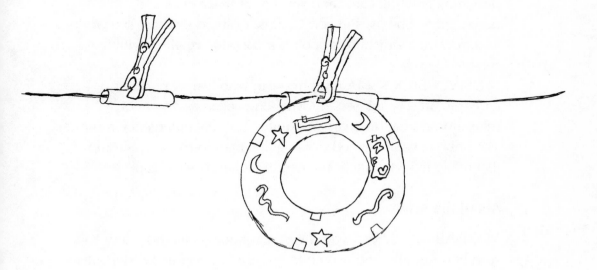

Your spaceships will slide across the string!

About the Authors

A former peace corps volunteer and teacher in high schools and colleges, MARY BLOCKSMA has written several children's books and textbook selections. Her accomplishments also include designing greeting cards and writing for magazines and newspapers. She lives in Fort Collins, Colorado, where she works as a freelance writer. This book is a cooperative effort with her brother Dewey.

DEWEY BLOCKSMA is a physician who is now pursuing a career in art. His interest in toymaking began as a form of relaxation during his years working in hospital emergency rooms. The hobby eventually led to designing easy-to-make spaceships that really fly! Mr. Blocksma lives in Holland, Michigan.

About the Artist

MARISABINA RUSSO, who lives in Yorktown Heights, New York with her husband and two children, is a talented and active artist. Her work has appeared on the cover of *The New Yorker* magazine and she illustrated another Prentice-Hall children's book, *Vegetables: An Illustrated History with Recipes.*